MW00580908

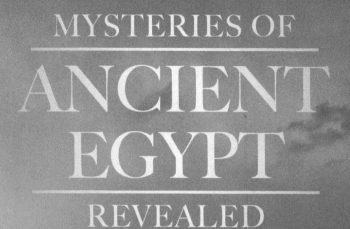

MYSTERIES OF
ANCIENT EGYPT

REVEALED

Children's Book on Egypt Grade 4
Children's Ancient History

BABY PROFESSOR
EDUCATION KIDS

First Edition, 2020

Published in the United States by Speedy Publishing LLC, 40 E Main Street, Newark, Delaware 19711 USA.

© 2020 Baby Professor Books, an imprint of Speedy Publishing LLC

Baby Professor Books are available at special discounts when purchased in bulk for industrial and sales-promotional use. For details contact our Special Sales Team at Speedy Publishing LLC, 40 E Main Street, Newark, Delaware 19711 USA. Telephone (888) 248-4521 Fax: (210) 519-4043. www.speedybookstore.com

10 9 8 7 6 * 5 4 3 2 1

Print Edition: 9781541953543
Digital Edition: 9781541956544

See the world in pictures. Build your knowledge in style.
www.speedypublishing.com

TABLE OF CONTENTS

Egypt is a land of mystery. The culture and history of ancient Egypt is so complex and fascinating that it has its own field of academic study, Egyptology. Famed Egyptologists have been working to unravel the mysteries of ancient Egypt and to learn how the people of ancient Egypt were able to make lasting contributions to mankind and build massive monuments that have stood the test of time. Let's take a closer look at the land of the pharaohs and pyramids, Sphinx and sarcophaguses, mummies and monuments.

PYRAMIDS IN DESERT OF
EGYPT

5

WHERE IS EGYPT?

Egypt is in the northern part of Africa, on the coast of the Mediterranean Sea.

Today, much of the country is a desert. In fact, it is located within the great Sahara Desert.

SAHARA DESERT

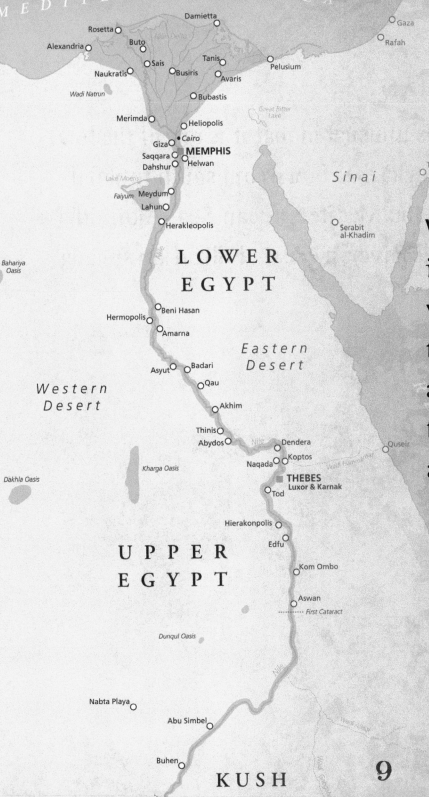

MEDITE

Rosetta
Alexandria
Damietta
Gaza
Rafah
Buto
Naukratis
Sais
Tanis
Busiris
Avaris
Pelusium
Wadi Natrun
Bubastis
Merimda
Heliopolis
Cairo
Giza
MEMPHIS
Saqqara
Dahshur
Helwan
Lake Moeris
Timna
Sinai
Faiyum
Meydum
Lahun
Herakleopolis
Serabit
al-Khadim
Bahariya
Oasis

LOWER
EGYPT

Nile

Beni Hasan
Hermopolis
Amarna
Eastern
Desert
Badari
Asyut
Western
Desert
Qau
Akhim
Thinis
Abydos
Nile
Dendera
Koptos
Naqada
Quseir
Kharga Oasis
THEBES
Luxor & Karnak
Dakhla Oasis
Wadi Hammamat
Tod

Hierakonpolis
Edfu
UPPER
EGYPT
Kom Ombo
Aswan
Bernike
First Cataract
Dunqul Oasis

Nile

Nabta Playa
Abu Simbel

Buhen
KUSH

Great Bitter
Lake

What makes Egypt unique is the Nile River, a major waterway that flows through the desert sands and provides a ribbon of fertile soil on its banks that are ideal for agriculture.

NILE RIVER

9

The Nile River is unusual in that it is one of the few rivers in the world that flow from south to north. It empties into the Mediterranean Sea. Along the shores of the Nile River, a great civilization sprang up.

NILE RIVER, ASWAN, EGYPT

WHO WERE THE EARLY EGYPTIANS?

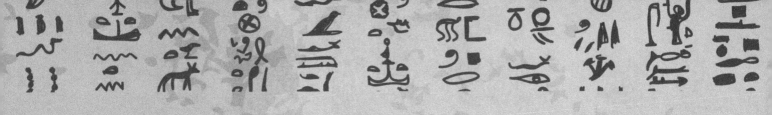

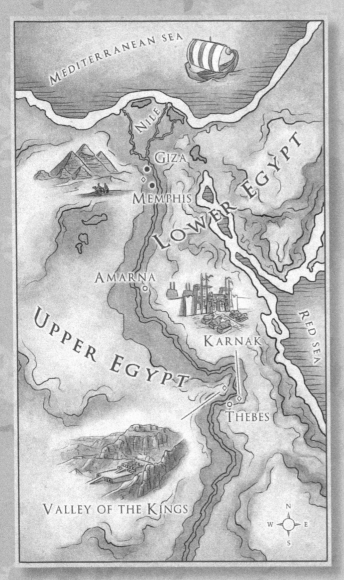

Long ago, there were actually two kingdoms in Egypt, one in Upper Egypt and one in Lower Egypt.

LOWER AND UPPER
EGYPT

The two kingdoms were united sometime around 3100 BC by the king of Upper Egypt, Menes, who wanted to rule over the entire region. Menes established the first Egyptian dynasty and his reign ushered in the beginning of the great Egyptian culture.

LIMESTONE HEAD OF
KING MENES

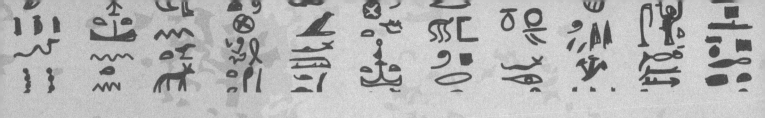

He formed a national government, instilled a sense of national pride in his people, and set the stage for the momentous construction projects that came in the following years.

A PALETTE OF KING MENES WITH DEFEATED ENEMY

THE GREAT PHARAOHS
OF EGYPT

In addition to Menes, there have been numerous great kings, or pharaohs, of Egypt. Pharaohs were more than ordinary kings. It was thought that they were truly gods who were living on Earth to rule the people.

A BUST OF A PHARAOH

The title of pharaoh was passed down from father to first born son, although there were a few notable female pharaohs in Egyptian history, including Hatshepsut, Nefertiti, and Cleopatra.

HATSHEPSUT

NEFERTITI

CLEOPATRA

One of the best-known pharaohs of ancient Egypt was Ramses II. He was important because he commissioned enormous building projects throughout his kingdom, including the temple of Abu Simbel that features four 60-foot statues in his likeness guarding the entrance to the temple.

RAMESSES II HOLDING A CROOK AND A FLAIL

EGYPT'S FIRST PYRAMIDS

Egypt is known for its iconic pyramids. Did you know there are more than thirty pyramids of varying sizes all up and down the Nile's west bank?

EGYPT IS FAMOUS FOR ITS
PYRAMIDS

THE STEP PYRAMID OF DJOSER IS LOCATED AT SAQQARA, SOUTH OF MEMPHIS

The royal pyramids were built to house the bodies of dead pharaohs and protect them on their journey to the afterlife. The first Egyptian pyramid was built sometime around 2650 B.C. by the pharaoh Zoser. This pyramid, Egyptologists theorize, served as a learning curve for future pyramids. This first pyramid was not smooth sided like subsequent ones but was a step pyramid. It still stands today at roughly 200 feet tall.

Another pyramid, which was started around 2600 BC by King Huni and completed by King Snefru, was built as a step pyramid, but then the sides were filled in and covered in limestone to give it a smooth appearance.

THE MEIDUM PYRAMID IN
EL WASTA, EGYPT

THE GREAT PYRAMID AT GIZA

The most well-known of all of Egypt's pyramids is the Great Pyramid at Giza. It is the only one of the Seven Wonders of the Ancient World that is still standing today.

PYRAMIDS OF GIZA

Its construction was ordered by King Khufu who wanted the largest and most impressive pyramid to serve as his tomb.

KING KHUFU

27

For more than 20 years, roughly between 2589 and 2566 B.C., a workforce of over 100,000 men, probably slaves, toiled to cut, move, and place approximately two and a half million giant stone blocks.

Originally, the Great Pyramid stood 481 feet tall - the tallest manmade structure for centuries - but some of the stones at the pinnacle[1] have fallen off. Today, the pyramid is only 450 feet high. It has a footprint that encompasses more than twelve acres.

1 Pinnacle – The highest point, the very top

THE GREAT PYRAMID

THE OTHER PYRAMIDS AT GIZA

The Great Pyramid is one of three large pyramids constructed on the Giza Plateau.

THE GREAT PYRAMID,
PYRAMID OF KHUFU

31

Joining it are the Pyramid of Khafre and the
Pyramid of Menkaure.

FIRST PYRAMID FROM THE LEFT: PYRAMID
OF MENKAURE
PYRAMID ON THE CENTER: PYRAMID OF
KHAFRE

33

The Pyramid of Khafre, the
second largest pyramid, was
built to be the tomb of the
pharaoh Khafre, who ruled
Egypt 4,500 years ago.

A noticeable feature of the Pyramid of Khafre is the cap of stone plaster that still remains at the peak of the structure. It gives researchers a fairly accurate idea of what the entire exterior of the pyramid once looked like.

PYRAMID OF KHAFRE

The Pyramid of Menkaure is the smallest of the three pyramids. Made of limestone and granite, it was completed in 2510 B.C. as the tomb to the pharaoh Menkaure of the 4th Egyptian dynasty.

PYRAMID OF
MENKAURE

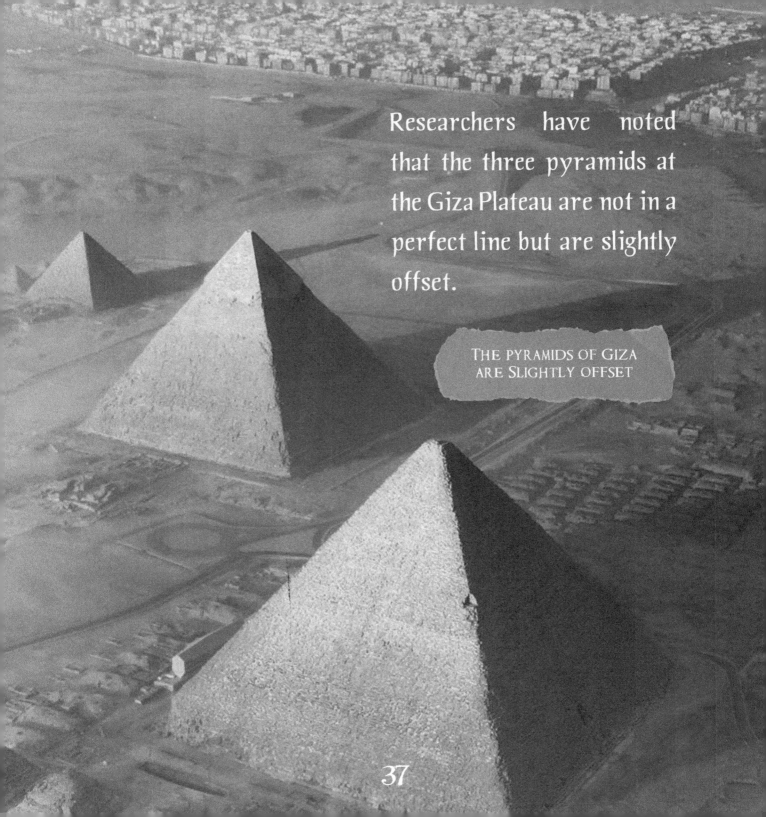

Researchers have noted that the three pyramids at the Giza Plateau are not in a perfect line but are slightly offset.

THE PYRAMIDS OF GIZA ARE SLIGHTLY OFFSET

They have noticed that the placement of the pyramids mirrors the three brightest stars in the constellation Orion, therefore there is speculation that the pyramid builders took inspiration from the night sky.

THE PLACEMENT OF THE PYRAMIDS OF GIZA MIRRORS THE THREE BRIGHTEST STARS IN THE CONSTELLATION ORION

WHAT IS INSIDE A PYRAMID?

If the pyramids were meant to be tombs for just one pharaoh, they are certainly big enough...too big, in fact.

STAIRWAY TOWARDS THE TOMB INSIDE THE PYRAMID OF KHAFRE

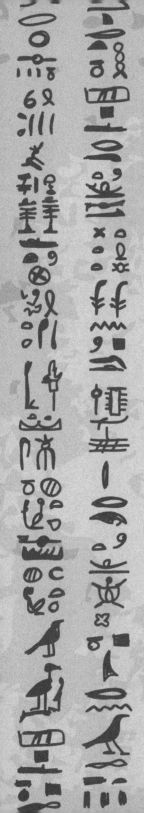

Inside a pyramid, however, archaeologists have found more than just the remains of one king. The pharaoh's personal possessions were also placed in the pyramid, along with treasures and items that would be handy in the afterlife, including food, games, clothing, tools, musical instruments, and sometimes even boats.

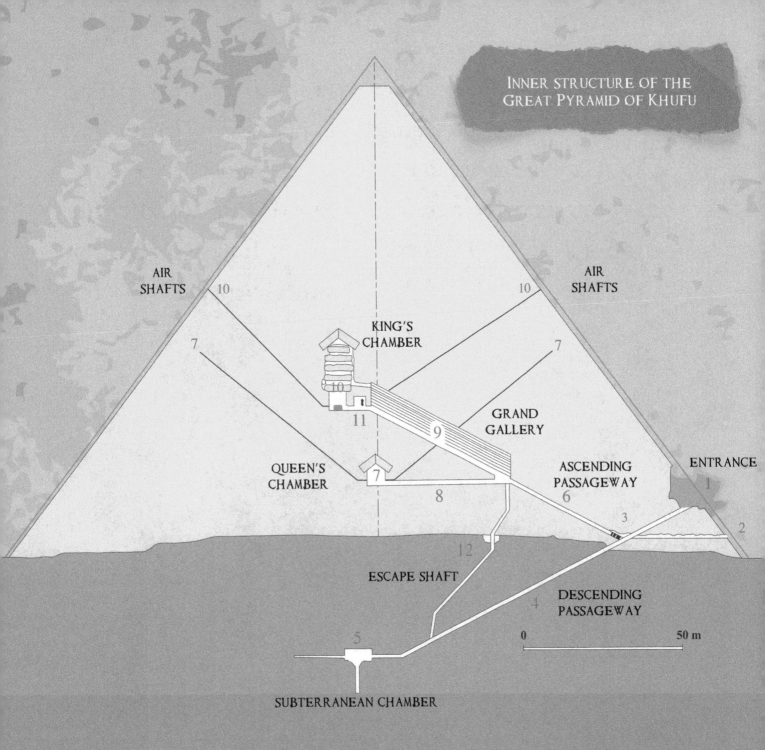

INNER STRUCTURE OF THE
GREAT PYRAMID OF KHUFU

AIR
SHAFTS
10

AIR
SHAFTS
10

7

7

KING'S
CHAMBER

10

11

9

GRAND
GALLERY

ENTRANCE

1

QUEEN'S
CHAMBER

7

8

ASCENDING
PASSAGEWAY

6

3

2

12

ESCAPE SHAFT

DESCENDING
PASSAGEWAY

4

0   50 m

5

SUBTERRANEAN CHAMBER

43

The king's family members and trusted servants may also be entombed with him. The ancient Egyptians were fearful of evil spirits who might prevent their dead king from reaching the afterlife, therefore they added winding tunnels and traps throughout the interior of the pyramid to trick the spirits.

A 3D RENDERING OF AN EGYPTIAN TOMB

HOW WERE THE PYRAMIDS BUILT?

The Egyptian pyramids are a marvel of ancient engineering. It is amazing that the ancient people were able to build such massive structures without modern tools and without large cranes to lift the heavy stones into place.

AN ARTIST'S CONCEPT OF HOW SLAVES BUILT PYRAMIDS IN ANCIENT EGYPT

Archaeologists do not know conclusively how the pyramids were built, but they have some viable theories. They believe that the stones were cut from a quarry and transported up the Nile on boats to a place very close to the construction site.

AN UP CLOSE PHOTO OF ONE OF THE GREAT PYRAMIDS OF GIZA

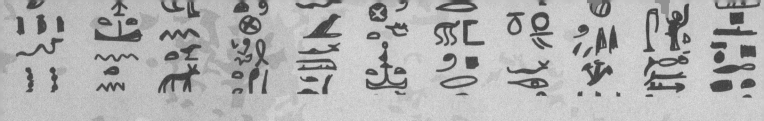

They think that the workers used wooden logs to roll the stones up earthen ramps to the appropriate level of the pyramid. Once the pyramid was complete, they believe, the dirt ramps were dismantled.

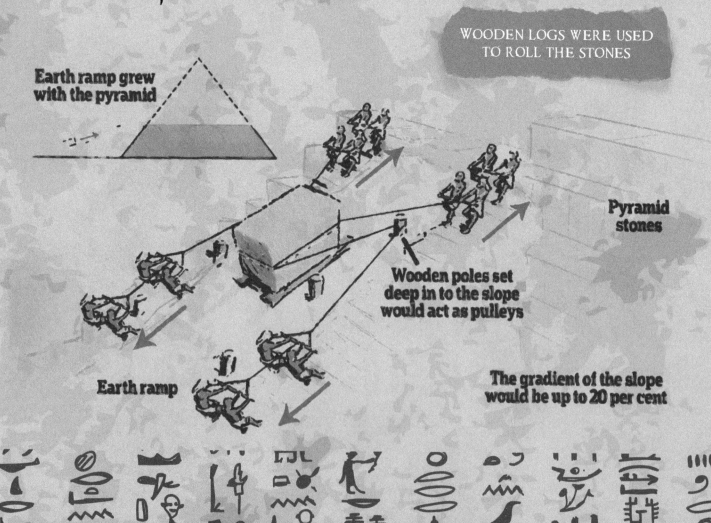

WOODEN LOGS WERE USED TO ROLL THE STONES

Earth ramp grew with the pyramid

Pyramid stones

Wooden poles set deep in to the slope would act as pulleys

Earth ramp

The gradient of the slope would be up to 20 per cent

THE ALL—KNOWING
SPHINX

Another giant symbol of Egypt is the ancient stone statue known as the Sphinx. Also located at the Giza Plateau, the statue represents a mythical animal that was said to have the body of a lion and the head of a human.

EGYPTIAN GREAT SPHINX.
GIZA. EGYPT

The statue, which is 240 feet long and more than 65 feet tall, was believed to have been carved during the reign of the pharaoh Khafre about 4,500 years ago and, according to archaeologists, the face is meant to be a likeness of the king.

THE SPHINX WAS CARVED DURING THE REIGN OF PHARAOH KHAFRE

At several points in its history, the Sphinx was swallowed up by the sands of the Sahara Desert until only its head was visible. That is why the head had suffered from the effects of wind, rain, and blowing sand more than the rest of the sculpture.

THE SPHINX HEAD SUFFERED
FROM THE EFFECTS OF THE WIND.
RAIN AND BLOWING SAND

THE WRITTEN
LANGUAGE OF THE
EGYPTIANS

Lining the walls of Egyptian tombs and temples are rows upon rows of intricate carvings of symbols, including birds, people, the sun, and the all-seeing eye.

ENGRAVINGS ON AN ANCIENT
EGYPTIAN TEMPLE WALL

At first, explorers thought that the symbols were simply artwork to adorn the walls and passageways. When more thorough studies of Egyptian temples began, Egyptologists began to wonder if the symbols were a system of writing, like pictographs.

ANCIENT EGYPTIAN WRITING

They called the Egyptian style of writing "hieroglyphics" because they thought the symbols stood for a combination of real and abstract concepts. The problem was that the last people who could read the hieroglyphics had died long ago. Egyptologists studying the writing could not discover its meaning. That is, until a lucky find helped them crack the writing.

MASSIVE COLUMNS WITH HIEROGLYPHICS, AND ANCIENT SYMBOLS IN KARNAK TEMPLE, EGYPT

THE ROSETTA STONE

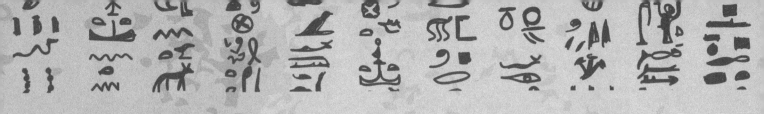

NAPOLEON BONAPARTE

On July 15, 1799, a group of soldiers from the army of Frenchman Napoleon Bonaparte stumbled upon a large stone slab in a town near the Nile River delta. The commanding officer immediately noticed something important about the slab - it had writing in three different writing systems on it.

The inscription was written in hieroglyphics, demotic, and Greek. The slab, dubbed the Rosetta Stone, was sent to England to be studied by linguists[2] and Egyptologists.

2 Linguist – A person who is skilled in different languages

ROSETTA STONE

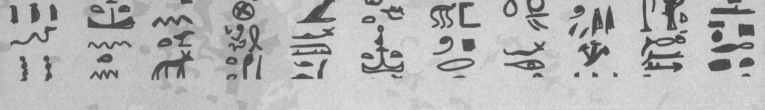

Because the other two writing styles were well known to scholars, they were able to uncrack the secrets to hieroglyphics and read not only the inscription on the Rosetta Stone, but all the inscriptions left on temples and tombs throughout ancient Egypt.

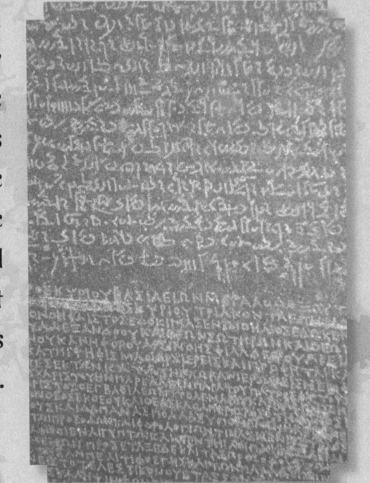

CLOSE UP SHOT OF THE ROSETTA STONE

EGYPT'S VALLEY OF THE KINGS

The belief in the afterlife was very important to the ancient Egyptians and they took many measures in life to ensure a rewarding afterlife. Although some kings were entombed in enormous pyramids, others were buried in hidden chambers cut into the rock in the Valley of the Kings.

The valley is located near the modern-day city of Luxor along the west bank of the Nile River.

Valley of the Kings

Cairo

Luxor

MAP SHOWING THE PROXIMITY OF THE VALLEY OF THE KINGS FROM THE CITY OF LUXOR IN EGYPT.

For about 500 years, from the 16th to the 11th century B.C., more than 60 royal tombs were dug into the valley and their entrances were hidden to protect them from grave robbers.

TOMB OF RAMESSES IV IN
VALLEY OF THE KINGS

Despite this measure, most of the tombs were raided and the treasures buried with the kings were stolen. That's what makes the discovery of the tomb of the boy pharaoh, Tutankhamen, so remarkable.

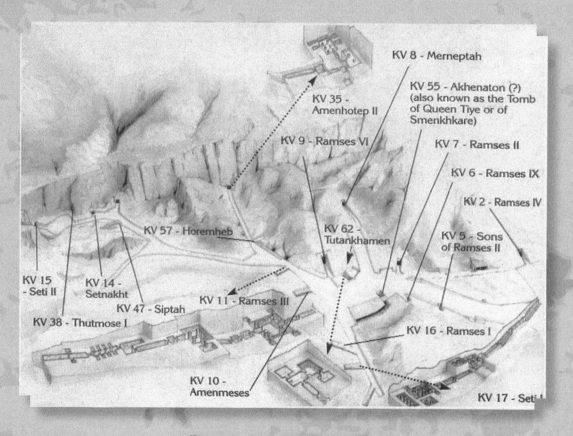

KV 8 - Merneptah

KV 35 - Amenhotep II

KV 55 - Akhenaton (?) (also known as the Tomb of Queen Tiye or of Smenkhkare)

KV 9 - Ramses VI

KV 7 - Ramses II

KV 6 - Ramses IX

KV 2 - Ramses IV

KV 57 - Horemheb

KV 62 - Tutankhamen

KV 5 - Sons of Ramses II

KV 15 - Seti II

KV 14 - Setnakht

KV 47 - Siptah

KV 11 - Ramses III

KV 16 - Ramses I

KV 38 - Thutmose I

KV 10 - Amenmeses

KV 17 - Seti

TOMBS OF VALLEY OF THE KINGS

KING TUT'S TOMB

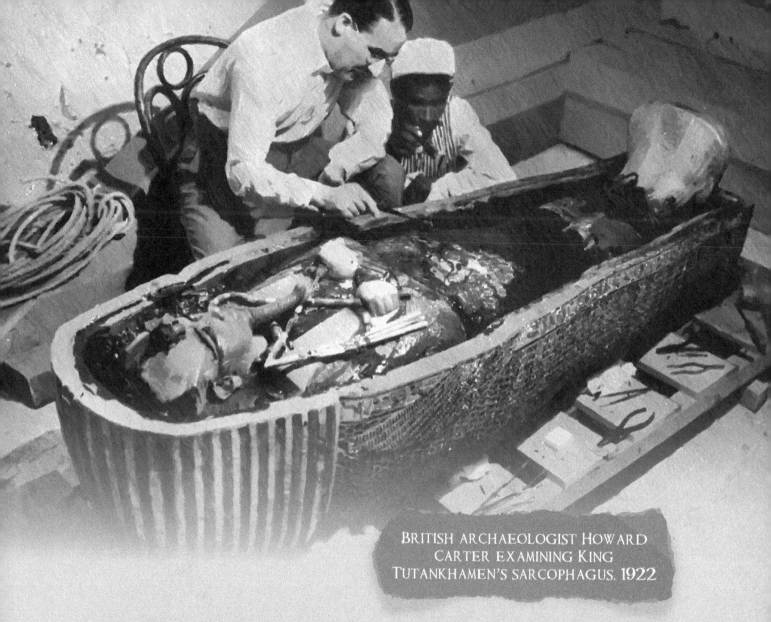

In 1922, British explorer and Egyptologist Howard
Carter and his team unearthed the long-hidden
entrance to King Tutankhamen's tomb.

70

King Tut, as he became known, ruled Egypt for a short time and died in 1352 B.C. at the age of only 18 years old. His tomb, which had been protected from grave robbers, was filled with gold artifacts[3] and jewels.

3 Artifact – A man made object, especially one that has been uncovered by archaeologists

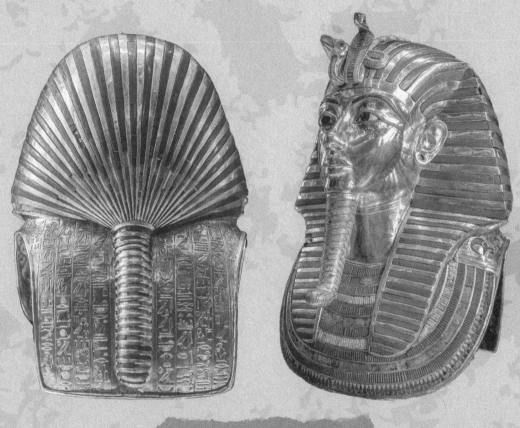

KING TUTANKHAMEN'S MASK
FRONT AND BACK

The mummified remains of the boy king were found in a gold sarcophagus, or coffin. The tomb was the most intact[4] burial chamber ever found of an Egyptian pharaoh and gave researchers insight into the life and funeral practices of the ancient Egyptians.

4 Intact – Whole, unaltered

BURIAL CHAMBER OF KING TUTANKHAMEN

EGYPTIAN MUMMIES

When a person died in ancient Egypt, particularly if that person was a royal, the body was carefully prepared to preserve it from decomposing[5] so that it was intact for the afterlife in a process called mummification.

5 Decomposing – Rotting, disintegrating

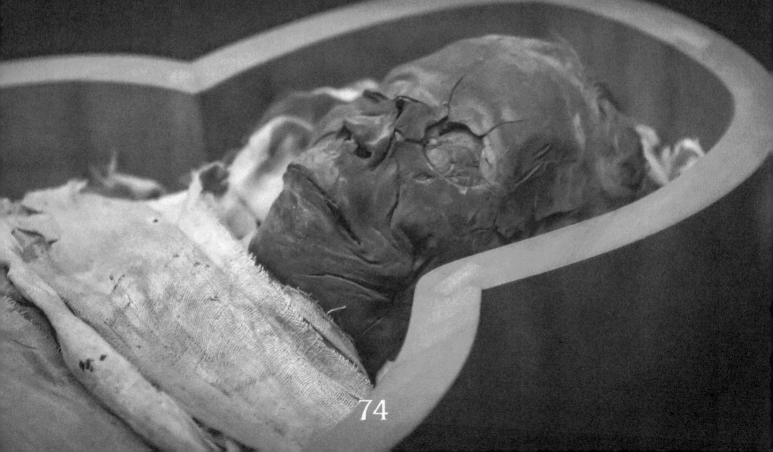

ANCIENT MUMMY IN THE SARCOPHAGUS

The process took more than two months to complete and was quite gruesome by today's standards. It involved extracting[6] the brain through the nostril and surgically removing all the organs except the heart. The body was then rubbed with oils and spices and allowed to dry out over a forty-day period.

6 Extract – To remove

MUMMIFICATION IN EGYPT

EGYPTIAN MUMMY

The last step was to tightly wrap the entire body in
thin strips of linen. Only then was the corpse ready
for burial.

SUMMARY

Ancient Egypt was a culture like no other on Earth. From the strange mummies to the towering pyramids, and from the mysterious Sphinx and the complex writing system, ancient Egypt tried to hold on to its secrets for centuries. Through the diligent work of Egyptologists, many of ancient Egypt's mysteries are no longer secret.

Many of history's ancient cultures were filled with mysteries and oddities. Now that you know about the mysteries of ancient Egypt, you should consider reading about other civilizations from long ago.

Visit

BABY PROFESSOR
EDUCATION KIDS

www.speedypublishing.com
to download Free Baby Professor eBooks
and view our catalog of new and exciting
Children's Books

CPSIA information can be obtained
at www.ICGtesting.com
Printed in the USA
LVHW050214170622
721517LV00006B/344